D0538380

# China

WITHDRAWN

**MEL FRIEDMAN**

**Children's Press®**
An Imprint of Scholastic Inc.
New York  Toronto  London  Auckland  Sydney
Mexico City  New Delhi  Hong Kong

**Content Consultant**
Ethan Michelson
Assistant Professor, Department of East Asian Languages and Cultures
Indiana University
Bloomington, Indiana

Library of Congress Cataloging-in-Publication Data

Friedman, Mel, 1946-
  China / by Mel Friedman.
        p. cm. -- (True book)
  Includes index.
      ISBN-13: 978-0-531-16852-3 (lib. bdg.)
              978-0-531-20726-0 (pbk.)
      ISBN-10: 0-531-16852-2 (lib. bdg.)
              0-531-20726-9 (pbk.)
  1. China--Juvenile literature. I. Title. II. Series.

  DS706.F75 2008
  951--dc22                              2007036025

Produced by Weldon Owen Education Inc.

1 2 3 4 5 6 7 8 9 10 R 17 16 15 14 13 12 11 10 09 08

# Find the Truth!

**Everything** you are about to read is true *except* for one of the sentences on this page.

Which one is **TRUE**?

**T or F**  The Great Wall of China can be seen from the moon.

**T or F**  Chinese writing can be read from top to bottom.

Find the answers in this book.

中國

# Contents

## 1 Think Big!

Which Chinese invention went off with a big bang? . . . 7

## 2 A Place of Wonders

What is known as the "Sea of Death"? . . . . . . . . . . 11

## 3 Son of Heaven

Which color were ordinary Chinese
people forbidden to wear? . . . . . . . 17

## THE BIG TRUTH!

## The Greatest Wall

What did guards in the Great Wall's
watchtowers look out for? . . . . . . . . 22

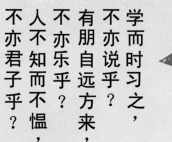

学而时习之，不亦说乎？有朋自远方来，不亦乐乎？人不知而不愠，不亦君子乎？

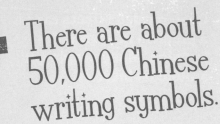

There are about 50,000 Chinese writing symbols.

**4 Strange but Beautiful**

What is so special about Chinese art and music? . . . . . . . . . . . . . . . . . . . **25**

**5 Chinese Ways**

Which animals were considered lucky in ancient China? . . . . . . . . . . **31**

**6 East Meets West**

What is the Mongolian Cow Yogurt Super Girl Contest? . . . . . . . . . . . . **37**

**True Statistics** . . . . . . . . . . **43**

**Resources** . . . . . . . . . . . . . **44**

**Important Words** . . . . . . . . **46**

**Index** . . . . . . . . . . . . . . . . **47**

**About the Author** . . . . . . . . **48**

Overcrowded streets can be a problem in some cities in China. Many people get around on bicycles.

6

# CHAPTER 1

# Think Big!

When you think about China, you have to think BIG! China has the world's largest population. More than one billion people live there. They come from 56 **ethnic** groups. China's written history and culture go back about 3,500 years. Today, China has one of the fastest-growing **economies** on the earth!

There are about 540 million bicycles in China!

In ancient China, soldiers flew noisy kites to frighten their enemies.

**The first kites were made from bamboo and silk. About 2,000 years ago, people in China began making kites from paper.**

## Leading the Way

Many inventions that changed the world came from China. Four famous ones are paper, the printing press, gunpowder, and the **compass**. The Chinese were the first to make silk. They were the first to make porcelain (POR-suh-lin) objects too. Porcelain is a hard, white ceramic. Kites and playing cards were also invented by the Chinese.

For centuries, China thought of itself as the center of the world. The Italian traveler Marco Polo reached China in 1274 A.D. He was amazed by its achievements in art and science. China's ruler welcomed Marco Polo. Later, rulers did not trust foreigners. They tried to close China's doors to foreigners and not trade with the world. Today, China welcomes visitors. Products made in China are sold all over the world.

**The Chinese ruler sent Marco Polo on many official tours of China.**

Traditional Chinese buildings have curved roofs. Many Chinese believed this shape scared off evil spirits.

# CHAPTER 2

# A Place of Wonders

China is part of eastern Asia. It has an area of 3.7 million square miles (9.6 million square kilometers). This is about the size of the United States. Its weather is also like ours. It is cold in the north and warm in the south. In China, the south and east are usually warmer and wetter than the north and west.

China has only one time zone. If you travel in China, you set your watch only once.

Fewer than 1,000 giant pandas live in the wild.

**China is home to many rare animals. Wild giant pandas live in the mountain forests of western and southwestern China.**

## China's Great Land

Western China is called the "Roof of the World." It has many towering mountains. The world's highest peak, Mount Everest, lies partly in China.

The Taklimakan (tah-kluh-muh-KAHN) Desert is in northwestern China. It is so dry that it is known as the "Sea of Death." Ancient traders built camel roads around it to transport silk to Europe. The Gobi (GOH-bee) is in northern China. It is one of the world's largest deserts.

China has two important rivers. The Huang He (hwahng huh) is China's second-longest river. It is found in the north. It is also called "China's Sorrow." It was given this nickname because it has flooded hundreds of times, killing millions of people.

China's Yangtze (yahng-dzuh) River is the longest river in Asia. It stretches for 3,900 miles (6,275 kilometers). Sugarcane, soybeans, tea, and rice grow along its banks.

Rice is one of the main foods of China. It grows well in wet fields.

CHINA

Beijing

Huang He River

Yangtze River

# A Changing China

About half of all the people in China have jobs connected to farming. But that is rapidly changing. Thousands of new factories have opened up. Millions of farmers have moved to the cities to find better jobs. In the past, young people were not allowed to choose their own jobs. The government decided for them. Now people in China have more freedom to pick their careers.

China is building the world's biggest dam on the Yangtze River in central China. The dam will create electricity. It will also control flooding.

China still faces big problems. Its cities suffer from terrible air pollution. Its factories sometimes dump harmful chemicals into its rivers. More than 150 million people live in poverty.

But China finally has enough food to feed its population. Many families have extra money to spend. All big cities have modern shopping centers, movie theaters, and supermarkets.

Red is a lucky color in China.
Yellow was a special color too.
Only the emperor and his family
could wear yellow.

# CHAPTER 3

# Son of Heaven

From 221 B.C. to 1912 A.D., the Chinese empire was ruled by more than 12 different **dynasties**. They were powerful rulers from the same family. The ruler of China was the **emperor**. The Chinese believed the emperor was chosen by their highest god. They called the emperor the "Son of Heaven."

In 2,000 years, China had 232 emperors.

The first emperor of China was named Qin Shi Huangdi (chin shirr hwong-dee).

# War and Power

Until the 1300s, China was the world's most advanced nation. Then it began to fall behind Japan and Europe. In the 1800s, China was attacked by Great Britain and other countries. The winners made China give them land and special trading rights. Many Chinese blamed their rulers for the defeats.

In 1912, **revolutionaries** forced the last emperor to give up power. Later, a civil war broke out to decide who would rule China. The war lasted until 1949, when the **Communists** took control of China. Mao Zedong (mow zeh-doong) became China's ruler.

**Pu Yi (poo yee) was the last emperor of China. He became emperor at the age of two. He was six when he gave up the throne. The emperor lived in the Forbidden City. It was called this because no one could enter or leave it without his permission.**

# China's Columbus

In 1405, a brave explorer named Zheng He (juhng huh) set sail from China to find new lands. For the next 28 years, he made seven voyages. He went as far as Africa. He fought pirates. He traded Chinese silks for spices, jewels, and rare animals. On one trip, he returned with a giraffe. China's emperor had never seen one before. He thought it was a mythical Chinese animal called the Qi Lin (chee lin). Zheng's voyages began almost a century before those of Christopher Columbus. His ships were many times bigger!

郑和宝船

ZHENG HE TREASURE BOAT
1405——1433

China is still a Communist country. Chinese people are not free to choose their own leaders. The government is run only by people who belong to the Communist Party. Ordinary people can get into trouble if they speak out against the government. In 1989, in Beijing, thousands of students and other protesters gathered peacefully. They wanted more freedom. Soldiers fired into the crowd. Hundreds of protesters were killed.

## China Time Line

**551 B.C.**
The great teacher Confucius (kuhn-FYOO-shuhss) is born.

**100s B.C.**
Silk is transported along the Silk Road. This was a series of trade routes between China and Europe.

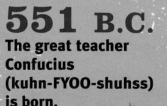

For a long time after Mao Zedong's victory in 1949, the United States and China were not on good terms. A turning point took place in 1972. Richard Nixon became the first U.S. president to visit the People's Republic of China. Nixon's trip made it possible for the United States and China to put aside their differences. Now the two countries are on friendly terms. Many people hope that this growing friendship will lead to more opportunities for the Chinese people.

**1971**
**China joins the United Nations. This is an international organization that promotes world peace.**

**1997**
**Britain returns Hong Kong to China.**

# The Greatest Wall

The Great Wall of China is the longest structure ever built by humans. It is about 4,500 miles (7,240 kilometers) long. The first emperor of China began building the wall in about 221 B.C. He wanted to keep enemies from the north out of his empire. The work on the wall continued off and on for hundreds of years.

## Help!

The Great Wall has about 25,000 watchtowers. When an enemy was about to attack, guards in the towers would light fires to send messages to other guards.

## Building It

The sides of the wall were built of bricks or stone. The wall was then filled with earth.

## Seen From Space?

For many years, people have believed that the Great Wall of China can be seen from the moon. Like many other structures, it can be seen from a low orbit of Earth. But it cannot be seen from the moon.

These clay soldiers were buried near the tomb of China's first emperor. No two faces on these statues are the same.

# CHAPTER 4

# Strange but Beautiful

Thousands of life-sized clay soldiers and horses have been uncovered near the tomb of the first emperor.

For ages, China had little contact with the rest of the world. It developed its own forms of art and music. Some Chinese arts, such as making silk and porcelain, later spread to the West. Other arts are still found only in China.

# Music and Drama

Ancient Chinese music often sounds strange to Western ears. That's because it uses a different scale. It has only five tones. Western music uses a scale with eight tones. Chinese notes are also different from Western notes.

**This Chinese violin has only two strings. It is played with a bow.**

The front of the sound box is covered with python skin.

Many people in China enjoy drama and theater. The most famous kind of drama is called Peking opera. It tells a story with song and dance. Performers wear colorful costumes and makeup. They dance and do amazing jumps.

Until the twentieth century, only men performed in Peking opera.

# The Art of Chinese Arts

Ancient Chinese masters painted watercolors
on silk and paper, as do many Chinese artists today.
Chinese paintings usually show scenes from nature.
Often they also have poems on them. That is
because the Chinese consider "beautiful writing,"
or **calligraphy**, an art too.

Some Chinese people believe that there are three national treasures: food, medicine, and **martial** (MAR-shuhl) **arts**, such as kung fu (kuhng foo) and tai ji (ty jee). Today in China, young and old practice these arts to strengthen

their minds and bodies. Martial arts were made popular in the West by movies of the famous Chinese actor Bruce Lee.

**These people are doing tai ji. There are hundreds of different kinds of martial arts.**

29

Confucius believed
that if everyone
showed respect
for others, society
would be at peace.

# CHAPTER 5

# Chinese Ways

For thousands of years, Chinese people have shared common beliefs. It is considered important to show respect, obedience, and loyalty to their family and society. The Chinese people owe many of these beliefs to Confucius. He was a famous and well-respected **philosopher**. He lived from about 551 B.C. to about 479 B.C.

Confucius said, "Do not do to others what you do not want done to yourself." This Golden Rule is part of most world religions.

# Speaking Chinese

The Chinese language has no alphabet. If you say the same sound with a different tone of voice, the meaning of the word changes. Written words are made up of **symbols**. These are called **characters**. Characters stand for ideas and things, rather than sounds. Chinese can be written from top to bottom, left to right, or right to left. However, it must be read in the same direction as it was written.

All people in China have one written language. But there are different ways of speaking Chinese. A person from northern China may not understand someone from the south. Mandarin became the official language of China because it was the language spoken in Beijing, the capital city.

Many Chinese believe the number eight is lucky. It sounds like the word for "to get rich."

八

Chinese children have to learn several thousand characters by heart. This girl is writing the words for "country" and "me."

国发

# Fireworks, Lions, and Dragons

In the West, people celebrate New Year's Day on January 1. However, the Chinese use a lunar calendar. Their New Year falls between January 21 and February 20. New Year is the most important Chinese holiday. It lasts for four days. Families get together for big meals. Some go on vacation.

**At the New Year, many children receive red envelopes with money inside.**

No Chinese New Year celebration is complete without loud fireworks, red lanterns, and dragon and lion dances. Dragons and lions are ancient signs of good luck. Fireworks are believed to scare away evil spirits from the old year.

The Internet helps connect
businesses, people, and ideas
from East and West.

# CHAPTER 6

# East Meets West

The Chinese government regulates the Internet. It even blocks some Web sites.

Today, young people in China live in a different world from that of their grandparents. China's economy is booming. Computers and the Internet have made information more accessible to more people. New opportunities exist for smart, hardworking people. Many children look forward to brighter futures than their parents did.

# Growing Up in China

Chinese students can go to college after 12 years of schooling. However, there are not enough openings for everyone. To win a place, students must take difficult tests. These include English-language exams.

In the 1900s, China's population grew very rapidly. There were too many people for the resources. Since the 1970s, people have been allowed to have only one child. Recently, in some parts of China, people have been allowed to have two children.

**Twins were exempt from the one-child policy.**

38

# Reaching for the Stars

Many young Chinese are proud of their country. In October 2003, they watched with excitement as China launched its first astronaut into space. China is also proud of its athletes who have made it big in the West. Perhaps the most famous is Yao Ming (yow ming). Yao is 7.5 feet (2.3 meters) tall. He is the center for the Houston Rockets. Yao is a national hero in his homeland.

Basketball is one of the most popular school sports in China.

## Popular China

The Chinese government tries to limit what young people can see and read. But the Internet and cell phones, as well as American movies, music, and TV shows, are slowly changing that. Cell phones are everywhere in China. Parents complain that their children spend too much time sending text messages and playing video games.

Four hundred million people watched the final Super Girl show. People voted for the winner by cell phone. ➡

In 2005, 120,000 Chinese girls signed up to sing in a TV talent contest like American Idol. The show was called the Mongolian Cow Yogurt Super Girl Contest. Super Girl quickly became the most popular TV show in China. On the final show, millions of viewers voted for the winner.

In 2005, Li Yuchun (middle) won the Super Girl contest. She received 3.5 million votes from fans throughout China.

The Chinese Olympic medals will be made from metal and jade.

# Going for Gold

In 2008, the Olympic Games will be held in China for the first time. For China, this is a great honor. It will be a chance to show the world the culture and spirit of the Chinese people.

For luck, the Olympics are scheduled to open on 8/8/08 at 8:08:08 P.M. China and the rest of the world will definitely be going for the gold! ★

# True Statistics

**Percentage of world population who live in China:**
About 20 percent

**Longest human-made waterway in the world:**
China's Grand Canal, 1,085 miles
(1,747 kilometers)

**World's largest rice producer:** China

**Largest group of palaces in the world:**
The Forbidden City in Beijing

**Largest city in China:** Shanghai, population
about 18.2 million

**Number of cities with more than one million people:**
Nearly 100

**Driest desert in Asia:** Taklimakan Desert

## Did you find the truth?

**F** The Great Wall of China
can be seen from the moon.

**T** Chinese writing can be read
from top to bottom.

# Resources

## Books

Brownlie, Alison. *China*. London: Hodder Wayland, 2006. World in Focus Series.

Cotterell, Arthur. *China*. London: Dorling Kindersley Limited, 2006. Eyewitness Series.

Fontes, Justine and Ron. *China*. New York: Children's Press, 2003. A to Z Series.

Hoyt-Goldsmith, Diane. *Celebrating Chinese New Year*. New York: Holiday House, 1999.

Keene, Carolyn. *The Chinese New Year Mystery* (Nancy Drew Notebooks, No. 39). New York: Aladdin, 2000.

Morley, Jacqueline. *You Wouldn't Want to Work on the Great Wall of China!* New York: Franklin Watts, 2006.

Waterlow, Julia. *China*. London: Hodder Wayland, 2006. Country Insights Series.

# Organizations and Web Sites

**Ancient Chinese Inventions**
www.columbia.edu/itc/eacp/japanworks/song/readings/
inventions_timeline.htm
Here you will find a time line of Chinese inventions.

**All you need to know about China**
www.kidskonnect.com/content/view/307/27
Here you will find links to many sites about China's history,
sights, and sports.

**Chinese New Year**
www.educ.uvic.ca/faculty/mroth/438/CHINA/
chinese_new_year.html
Find out how Chinese New Year is celebrated.

# Places to Visit

**The Palace Museum**
(in the Forbidden City)
4 Jingshan Qianjie 100009
Beijing, China
+86 10 8511 7041
www.dpm.org.cn
See the art and architecture
of the Forbidden City.

**Asian Art Museum**
200 Larkin Street
San Francisco, CA 84102
(415) 5813500
www.asianart.org
View artwork from the Asian
continent, including Chinese
porcelain, jade, and calligraphy.

# Important Words

**calligraphy** (kuh-LIG-ruh-fee) – the art of decorative handwriting done with a brush or pen

**character** – a mark or symbol in a writing system

**Communist** (KOM-yuh-nist) – a type of government that believes land, houses, and businesses belong to the government or community, and the profits are shared by all

**compass** (KUHM-puhss) – a device that helps determine location and direction by use of a magnetic needle

**dynasty** (DYE-nuh-stee) – a series of rulers from the same family

**economy** – the system in which goods and services are produced, bought, and sold

**emperor** – a leader who holds the power over a country or a group of countries

**ethnic** – relating to people who are of the same race or culture, or who speak the same language

**martial art** – a sport that is a form of self-defense or attack

**philosopher** (fih-LOSS-uh-fer) – a person who studies truth, wisdom, and the nature of reality

**revolutionary** (rev-uh-LOO-shuhn-air-ee) – a person who wants to throw out a government by force

**symbol** (SIM-buhl) – an object that stands for something else

# Index

Page numbers in **bold** indicate illustrations

astronaut, 39

basketball, **39**
bicycles, **6–7**
buildings, **10**, **16**

calligraphy, **28**
children, **33**–34, 37–**38**, 40
Chinese New Year, **34–35**
clay soldiers, **24**–25
Columbus, Christopher, 19
Communism, 18, 20
compass, 8
Confucius, **20**, **30**–31

dam, **14–15**
dragons, 34–35

economy, 7, 37
education, 38
emperors, **9**, **16–17**, **18**–19, 23–25
envelopes, **34**

factories, 14–15
farming, 14
Forbidden City, 18

Gobi, 12
Great Wall, the, **22–23**
gunpowder, 8

Hong Kong, **21**
Huang He River, 13

Internet, **36**–37, 40

kites, **8**

language, 32–**33**, 38
lanterns, **35**
lion dance, **35**

Mandarin, 32
Mao Zedong, 18, 21
martial arts, **29**
medicine, 29
Mount Everest, 12
music, 25, **26–27**, 40–**41**

Olympic Games, **42**
opera, **27**

painting, **28**
pandas, **12**
paper, 8, 28
playing cards, 8
Polo, Marco, **9**
population, 7, 15, 38
porcelain, 8, 25
printing press, 8

rice, **13**

silk, 8, 12, 19–**20**, 25, 28
soybeans, 13
sugarcane, 13

Taklimakan Desert, 12
tea, 13
time zone, 11

United Nations, 21

violin, **26**

wars, 18
weather, 11
writing, **28**, 32–**33**

Yangtze River, 13, **14–15**

Zheng He, **19**

# About the Author

Mel Friedman is an award-winning journalist and children's book author. He has four graduate degrees from Columbia University, including one in East Asian studies. He also holds a B.A. in History from Lafayette College.

Friedman has written or co-written more than two dozen children's books, both fiction and nonfiction. He speaks and reads Chinese, and spent a year in China teaching English at Beijing Normal University's branch campus in Zhuhai, Guangdong Province.

**PHOTOGRAPHS** © 2008: Big Stock Photo: Mario Tomic (p. 7); Getty Images (cover, p. 19; pp. 22–23; p. 29; p. 33; p. 41); iStockPhoto.com: Blackredcards.com (p. 3); Hector Joseph Lumang (p. 43); Martijn Mulder (p. 26); Photolibrary (p. 8); Stock.XCHNG: Bryon Hardy (p. 5); Dieter Vander (Hong Kong, p. 21); Jari Lehtikangas (ball, p. 39); Randell Hop (p. 20); Richard Mallinson (p. 40); Stockxpert: Andrey Zyk (United Nations logo, p. 21); Tranz: Corbis (p. 6; p. 9; pp. 12–16; p. 24; p. 27; p. 30; p. 36; twins, basketball players, pp. 38–39; p. 42); Reuters (p. 10; p. 35)

The publisher would like to thank To Suen Lam for the painting on page 28.